Original title:
The House of Quiet Shadows

Copyright © 2025 Creative Arts Management OÜ
All rights reserved.

Author: Robert Ashford
ISBN HARDBACK: 978-1-80587-191-0
ISBN PAPERBACK: 978-1-80587-661-8

Whispered Wishes in the Air

In a nook where giggles creep,
Whispers tumble, secrets leap.
Cat in a hat, what a sight!
Chasing dust bunnies in the night.

Creaking floorboards sing a tune,
While mice dance under the moon.
A ghost with a grin, makes us laugh,
Juggling shadows on the path.

Through curtain veils, dreams sneak by,
Tickling noses, oh my, oh my!
A painting winks, with a sly grin,
Telling tales of the fun within.

In corners hid, a mystery waits,
Laughter blooms like open gates.
With every wish, the world appears,
A festival of giggles here!

The Comfort of Fading Echoes

In corners where whispers dare to play,
A sock puppet winks, then runs away.
Laughter creeps softly, intent to tease,
While shadows engage in a comical freeze.

The echoes all giggle, a mischievous crew,
As dust bunnies bounce, say 'How do you do?'
A clattering teapot joins in the fun,
While chairs sway and twirl as if they could run.

Portraits in Dimness

Frames hang adorned with faces so bright,
Yet they frown and grimace, oh what a sight!
A mustached cat takes center stage,
Striking poses, it fuels the mirage.

The glow in the corner seems ready to laugh,
As a painting spills secrets in a whimsical half.
Candlesticks wobble, a quirky ballet,
Dancing in shadows, they sigh and sway.

Traces of a Lingering Past

Cobwebs weave tapestries of silly lore,
Where socks disappear and come back for more.
A hovering hat, tipsy and spry,
Winks to the dust motes as they float by.

The clock chimes in with a giggle of time,
As shoes step lightly, in rhythm and rhyme.
Echoes of laughter from years long gone,
Play hide and seek with the light of dawn.

The Stillness That Remembers

In silence, there's mischief, a plot well laid,
While the old armchair croaks, 'Come dance, don't fade!'

The rugs whisper tales of prancing feet,
As the stillness chuckles, it can't be beat.

Beneath the floorboards, a tap-tap parade,
With giggles of children, in fun unafraid.
A game of charades with a ghostly twist,
In stillness, the laughter is hard to resist.

Twilight's Embrace of Solitude

In a room where dust bunnies play,
The shadows dance, they sway and sway.
A cat chases whispers on the wall,
While ghosts share jokes through the hall.

The clock ticks slow, I'm far from stressed,
In pajamas, I feel truly blessed.
With a muffin and tea on a plate so grand,
I'm the queen of this quiet land.

Untold Stories in Every Crack

Every crack in the wall has a tale to tell,
Of a shoe that got stuck in mischief so well.
The mouse found a treasure, a half-eaten pie,
While the spiders made webs that reach for the sky.

Lurking behind the curtains, they peek,
A sly grin from the floorboards, oh what a cheek!
As the candle flickers, laughter fills the air,
It's a camaraderie, slightly beyond compare.

Calm Reflections of an Unspoken Past

In the mirror hangs a quirky ghost,
Who offers sweet riddles, we laugh the most.
Battered chairs squeak with each passing breeze,
As secrets unfold under old, creaky eaves.

A sock lost in time is now quite a star,
It audibly chuckles, 'I've traveled so far!'
With laughter echoing in every nook,
I'll pen down the jokes in an old, dusty book.

Starlit Reveries

Under moonbeams, the shadows play pranks,
A raccoon in pajamas, giving me thanks.
Fireflies twinkle like stars on the ground,
As laughter rings out, in merriment sound.

A blanket of laughter feels cozy and bright,
It's a circus of giggles in the calm of the night.
As dreams spin like tops, in this silent fest,
The heart finds its rhythm, and smiles manifest.

Murmured Secrets of the Night

In the dark where shadows play,
Squeaky floorboards laugh and sway.
A cat's meow escapes the door,
While spoons jump for a midnight score.

Ghosts gossip with the creaking beams,
Sharing tales of forgotten dreams.
The clock chimes in a silly tune,
As dust bunnies dance beneath the moon.

Shadows Tucked in Corners

In every nook, a shadow looms,
Trying on its funniest costumes.
Worn-out shoes and mismatched socks,
Conjuring laughs, like silly flocks.

A table lamp winks, flickers bright,
While curtains whisper jokes at night.
The ghost of laughter fills the air,
As the vacuum swallows all despair.

Whispers of the Lingering Past

Old chairs creak with secrets told,
Of past antics, bold and gold.
The mirror grins at the shenanigans,
Reflecting smiles from old mannequins.

Time-traveling shoes with laces untied,
Dragging stories from the other side.
Ticklish memories float on by,
As the hallway echoes every sigh.

Silent Portraits of Time

Frames hanging askew, with a twitch,
Portraits laugh, sharing a glitch.
A sly grin from a mustached chap,
Tells knock-knock jokes from this old map.

They nod and wink as the chandeliers sway,
Catching giggles that waltz away.
In this gallery of the absurd,
Every whisper is beautifully blurred.

Silhouettes Against the Walls

In corners where the dust balls roll,
The silhouettes dance, stealing the soul.
A cat with a hat, oh what a sight,
Gossips with shadows 'til deep in the night.

A chair takes a nap, the rug starts to giggle,
Whispering secrets that make me wiggle.
The walls have their stories, both funny and frail,
While the cuckoo clock's telling its own little tale.

Echoes from the Corner of Time

Tick tock says the clock, with a wink and a nudge,
It echoes old jokes, no one can judge.
A mouse with a mustache, oh what a tease,
Pops out of shadows with ease and with cheese.

The whispers of laughter in spaces so tight,
Makes evening feel cozy, a friendly delight.
Time frolics by, skipping just like a kid,
Leaving puns behind, oh how they hid!

Lanterns in the Twilight

The lanterns swing low, casting giggles of light,
As shadows dance round, what a funny sight!
A ghost with a grin, dropped his sheet in a rush,
Tripped on the dog, oh, what a big hush!

The bats join the party, with jokes in their beaks,
Stirring up mischief, and laughter it seeks.
In the twilight they shimmer, all sparkly and grand,
Creating a spectacle, just as they planned.

Whispers of Worn Out Floors

The floors creak and groan, as they share their tales,
Of errant socks and runaway pails.
A floorboard winks, says, 'I heard you last night!'
'Was that a snack thief or a sneaky sprite?'

In every old split, a joke finds its way,
Through laughter and crackles, they dance and they play.
The dusty beams giggle, so full of delight,
Telling their stories til the morning's light.

Hushed Conversations with Time

In corners where dust bunnies play,
A clock laughs in its own quirky way.
Whispers float like a feathered tune,
While socks dance like they're on the moon.

Chairs tell secrets in creaky tones,
While a cat scampered over old bones.
Time skips and hops with a cheeky grin,
In this cozy realm where giggles begin.

The Palette of Twilight Shadows

Dusk spills colors from a tipped tray,
As shadows giggle and dance in gray.
The walls wear a cloak of playful night,
While the moon offers popcorn, what a sight!

Brushstrokes of laughter paint the air,
As fireflies gossip without a care.
Glimmers of joy twinkle like stars,
In a canvas where silliness never mars.

Crumbling Walls and Silent Hearts

The crumbling walls have stories to tell,
Of a ghost that's stuck in a cheerful spell.
Echos of laughter bounce off the stone,
As memories play like a well-tuned drone.

A creak in the floor makes laughter swell,
As the chandelier jiggles—can you tell?
Silent hearts thump in a rhythmic cheer,
In this place where silliness is near.

Serenity in the Shadows' Embrace

Shadows carry tales in their swirling dance,
As calmness invites you to take a chance.
A whisper of joy floats through the air,
While the floorboards chuckle without a care.

In corners where mischief takes a nap,
And laughter slips through the tiniest gap.
Serenity wraps its arms around,
In this whimsical silence, joy is found.

Footprints in the Quietude

In corners where giggles dance,
Old boots make a clumsy prance.
Dust bunnies roll with glee,
As they plot their next spree.

Socks have gone on a spree,
Chasing dreams wildly, you'll see.
Under the bed, they conspire,
With crumbs from last night's fire.

The clock chimes a quirky tune,
As the cat tries to swoon.
A dance of shadows does play,
Under the moon's soft ray.

In this place, laughter hides,
Behind the curtains it slides.
With each creak and every tune,
Life's a silly cartoon.

Shadows of Yesterday

Old whispers wink and nod,
As dust settles like a facade.
With walls that chuckle and coo,
Memories march in a queue.

A broom leans like a wise sage,
Reciting tales from age to age.
Murphy's law is at work,
As the fridge starts to twerk.

Doors creak with a knowing grin,
While chairs plot how to spin.
The shadows slide with a dash,
In this room of merry ash.

With whispers of laughter's song,
In this quiet, nothing feels wrong.
Between the sighs and grins,
Joyously, the chaos begins.

Veiled Realms of Rest

Behind curtains made of dreams,
Lurks an army of quirky memes.
Pillows giggle in delight,
Holding secrets of the night.

The coffee pot hums a tune,
While spoons dance with the moon.
A lazy cat sprawls with flair,
Chasing shadows through the air.

In stillness, the laughter waits,
Like a party of old mates.
Grand tales of days gone past,
With echoes that forever last.

Between the books' quiet sweep,
A mischievous laugh takes a leap.
In the realm of sleepy sighs,
Adventure in silence lies.

Notes from the Corner of Sighs

A chair in the corner, quite sly,
Watches as time flutters by.
Jokes tumble from shadows afar,
Guided by an unseen star.

A spider weaves tales of jest,
In a web that's completely blessed.
With threads of laughter so bright,
It's a party every night.

The teapot whistles a grin,
As the spoons decide to spin.
Every creak tells a tale,
Of frolics in a dusty veil.

In this nook, the light plays tricks,
With flickers that dance and mix.
Sighs may echo from the past,
But joy in the moment will last.

Fleeting Moments of Solitude

In corners where the dust bunnies play,
A sock dances in a cheerful ballet.
The clock mocks time with its tickle and chime,
Whispers of laughter in moments sublime.

A sandwich waits like a long-lost friend,
Cheese smiles, inviting me to descend.
While shadows giggle and shadows tease,
Caught in their games, I'm tickled with ease.

The cat takes a nap, dreaming bizarre,
A mouse wears a hat, driving a car.
In solitude's grasp, we play hide and seek,
With each silly thought, the quiet grows chic.

In this haven of calm, I chuckle and sigh,
The mundane turned merry, oh me, oh my!
For in this stillness, a symphony plays,
Fleeting moments that dance through my days.

Twilight's Embrace on Worn Walls

The twilight casts shadows, they waltz on the floor,
A chair creaks softly, asking for more.
As the old lamp hums a tuneful refrain,
Its flickers keep secrets hidden in grain.

Mismatched plates smile under dust's gentle clutch,
They're discussing their lives with a laugh and a touch.
Each whisper of color, a story long told,
The walls would join in if they weren't so old.

A lone spider spins a glittery thread,
Crafting odd tales of the guests who once tread.
In the hush, you can hear giggles resound,
As twilight embraces the quirks we've found.

With each passing moment, the laughter takes flight,
Turning silence to joy on this whimsical night.
Worn walls stand witness to the love that unrolls,
In a dance of soft shadows, they cradle our souls.

The Language of Quietude

In whispers of noon, where the daisies dare,
A ballet of shadows flits through the air.
Laughter blooms softly near the tired old chair,
Even the silence has stories to share.

A mug raises its rim, toasting dreams of yore,
While the cookies conspire for a sprinkle encore.
The fridge hums a tune, both sweet and absurd,
As the memories flutter, each seemingly blurred.

Dust motes are dancers in the sun's gentle hold,
Spinning around tales that are pieced and retold.
In the quiet, you'll find a chorus, a cheer,
For the language of stillness is perfectly clear.

So let the serene tickle your funny bone's tease,
In the midst of the calm, you can dance just like these.
Where glances and giggles compose quite a song,
In the hush of the moment, you'll find where you belong.

Reveries in the Gloom

Draped in shadows, the sofa reclines,
While pillows conspire, drawing silly designs.
A bat flits nearby, with a wink and a twist,
Casting spells of whimsy in the misty abyss.

Old books whisper tales, as pages take flight,
In the glow of a lantern, they dance through the night.
With ghosts of giggles floating about,
The house hums a tune, there's no hint of doubt.

As lanterns flicker, one steals a glance,
Surprising the curtains with a bold little dance.
In the gloom, there's a laughter that brightly resumes,
As the spirit of mischief stealthily looms.

In this reverie haunt, where echoes are sweet,
Every creak is a chuckle, each shadow's a treat.
So let's tiptoe softly and give a wide grin,
For the gloom holds delights, let the fun now begin!

Secrets Beneath the Floorboards

In a room where dust bunnies dare,
Lies a stash of old socks, beware!
They giggle and whisper when night falls,
Plotting their escape past the walls.

Under the boards, they hold a ball,
Dancing with crumbs and forgotten small,
With each creak, they hide their stash,
Chasing the cockroaches in a flash.

They trade tales of the lost TV remote,
And pass the time on a broken boat,
Each laugh echoes through cracks anew,
Waiting for someone to stumble through.

Why so silent, when fun's abound?
Just a few cat toys might make a sound,
In the shadows, the secrets gleam,
Nightly adventures, like a dream.

Murmurs of the Absent Light

In corners where the light forgot,
A dust mote parade is getting hot,
They whisper secrets, all in jest,
Like gossipy tales from a feathered nest.

Flickering bulbs, they giggle too,
Mocking the bravest ghost they knew,
With shadows performing a soft ballet,
In this silent rave, they laugh and play.

The moon takes the stage, dressed in white,
As glowing orbs compete for the light,
Spinning tales of silliness past,
Each twinkle a wink, so bright, so fast.

Who would have thought that silence could brawl,
When echoes of laughter could fill the hall?
In the absence of light, where whims take flight,
The shadows dance on, in sheer delight.

Shadows That Dance at Dusk

As the sun waves goodbye to the day,
Shadows emerge in a merry ballet,
They kick up their feet on a faulty chair,
With a shimmy and shake, they declare, 'We're here!'

A cat chases after a rogue beam,
Twisting and turning as if in a dream,
While the couch whispers secrets old,
Of clumsy pranks that never get told.

The fridge hums a tune, slightly off-key,
Joining the revelry, lost in glee,
Socks start spinning in whimsical flight,
Under the glow of a dim evening light.

Under the stars, they tumble and twist,
Each jolly jive not a moment missed,
For at dusk, when the world's feeling bold,
Even shadows have stories to unfold.

The Silence Between Breath

In the hush where whispers play hide and seek,
Lurks a valley of giggles, oh so unique,
It's a haven for odd socks, a sneaky pair,
Counting the moments when nobody's there.

Tickling the air with mischief untold,
The walls hold the laughter, bold yet controlled,
As silence stretches, the mischief grows,
Invisible pranks in the night softly show.

Each breath a pause, like a game so sly,
Wondering when laughter will soar and fly,
With echoes of chuckles reverberating near,
As the clock chimes funny tunes that we hear.

What secrets are kept in the spaces between?
As playful shadows recite the unseen,
In the silence of night, let the laughter spread,
For in every breath lies a joke to be said.

Murmurs from the Hearth

In corners where dust bunnies dance,
A cat named Whiskers takes his chance.
The kettle sings, though no one's near,
While ghosts play cards, they'll take your beer.

A creak of stairs, a light that winks,
A friendly chair that rarely shrinks.
With shadows peeking, potions brewed,
This place is cozy, not for the shrewd.

The picture frames are giggling low,
As everyone's knees begin to show.
The laughter lingers, sweet and sly,
While the bread rolls plot, oh my, oh my!

The fireplace grins, it's quite a scene,
Where mischief brews, and laughter's keen.
In whispers soft, the oddball crew,
Turns quiet nights to something new.

Timeless Hollows

In forgotten nooks where echoes cling,
Old chairs are humming, oh what a swing!
Forgotten secrets boast and brag,
While the lamp post plays a sad old drag.

Mice in hats throw a fancy ball,
But wind-up toys just trip and fall.
With every tick of a dusty clock,
The shadows giggle, what a shock!

Candles flicker, what a jest,
The flick of tongues, like a tiny fest.
Dust motes jive in the soft moonlight,
While the curtains sway with sheer delight.

Beneath the stairs, the poltergeist craves,
To know which sock, the laundry saves.
These timeless hollows, a comical sight,
Turn quiet moments into pure delight.

Gaze into the Fading Light

As twilight drapes its soft embrace,
The oddest shapes begin to race.
A broom takes off, it knows the way,
While shadows laugh at end of day.

The old TV cracks a silly joke,
While my tea sips from the mischievous oak.
A portrait winks with devilish glee,
In the fading light, we're all carefree.

Chairs spin round like wild, lost souls,
As mismatched socks pull off their roles.
The lightbulbs flicker, "Just one more dance!"
In twilight's heart, we take our chance.

With every creak, the world stands still,
As laughter bubbles, we sip and spill.
A gathering of curious sights,
In the sweet embrace of fading lights.

Gentle Lull of the Unseen

In stillness where soft whispers flit,
A vacuum sighs, it's having a fit.
The curtains twirl in gentle waves,
As secrets hide in glassy enclaves.

A tick-tock rhythm plays a game,
While the fridge hums its hungry fame.
The floorboards gossip, soft and meek,
In the lull of night, the silence squeaks.

From shadows rise the quirkiest dreams,
With sideways glances, and silly schemes.
A jester's hat tries on for size,
In the unseen, the fun complies.

So come along, join in the fun,
As the clock strikes twelve, we're not yet done.
A gentle lull, a playful tease,
Where laughter drips like evening breeze.

Whispers in the Stillness

In corners where the dust bunnies play,
Tales of old silliness linger and sway.
A sock goes missing, a shoe on a spree,
In the quiet, it chuckles—oh, what can it be!

A creak in the floorboards, a giggle so sly,
Chairs dance with laughter, oh my, oh my!
A ghost with a tickle, a brush on the neck,
Time flies with a wink—this place is a wreck!

Whispers of mischief float soft in the air,
While shadows play tag without any care.
A cat yawns its stories; it leans on the wall,
As curtains conspire in a grand, silly ball.

So come out of hiding, join in the fun,
In echoes and giggles, we're never quite done.
For in this stillness, bright humor takes flight,
You'll find joy in the shadows, both day and night!

Echoes of Forgotten Corners

In nooks where the old broom has gathered its dust,
Echoes of laughter arise, just because.
A forgotten old trinket winks cheekily bright,
Reminding us all that the fun's in the light.

A rogue rubber chicken sits under the chair,
With wisdom to share, it's seen everywhere.
It cackles at shadows that flit past the wall,
And claims it was hiding—oh, what fun for all!

The clock has its secrets, tick-tocking away,
But jests hidden there don't want to decay.
Let's lift up the cushions, let's peek 'neath the drapes,
For giggles are waiting in hilarious shapes.

So gather your friends in this echoing space,
Where fun meets the quiet, a curious place.
Laughter and whispers intertwine with the night,
In corners forgotten, we find pure delight!

Veils of Dust and Memory

Beneath layers of dust, old tales start to play,
With giggles embedded in ceilings of gray.
A cat on the mantle, it snores with a grin,
Dreaming of antics it's been stubborn in.

Old pictures are laughing, their smiles dusted gold,
They mingle with echoes, each story retold.
A fish on the wall gives a wink, just for fun,
Claiming it's won every race—surely none!

A specter in slippers shuffles back to the light,
Stumbling on memories, all in delight.
Ghostly chortles echo through misty old halls,
As laughter unravels, and joy freely calls.

So let's dust off the corners, invite in the cheer,
Where shadows feel lighter, and fun isn't queer.
The veils of old memory keep mischief intact,
In every soft echo, a joy in the act!

Solitude in the Timeless Halls

In halls that stretch onward, where quiet will reign,
Solitude giggles, dismissing the sane.
A door creaks open, it chuckles with glee,
As if to say, 'Come play hide-and-seek with me!'

The walls are alive with the stories they share,
With whispers and tickles dancing in air.
Your shadow starts prancing, it sneaks on your heel,
In this solitude, laughter becomes most surreal.

A cushion musters courage, it springs from its spot,
Proclaiming itself as an elegant lot.
While old furniture grumbles in laughter and ache,
The silence becomes a grand spectacle of make!

So wander the timeless, the halls never cease,
Invite in the silly, find laughter and peace.
For in solitude's company, joy's deeply found,
In the echoing stillness, hilarity's crowned!

Whispers Across the Threshold

In corners where the dust bunnies play,
A sock with no match plots its escape.
The fridge hums a tune, oh so gray,
As a cat takes a nap on its favorite drape.

Old chairs creak secrets of laughter and sighs,
While curtains flirt gently with the breeze.
A light bulb flickers, rolling its eyes,
As ghostly tales dance with mischievous ease.

A shadow winks, saying, 'Not quite my time,'
While slippers plot mischief, sly as a fox.
Their jumbled adventures, a comical rhyme,
Echo through hallways, old as the clocks.

So raise a glass to the silliness found,
In the nooks of this laughter-infused space.
For every hush hides a giggle profound,
And every creak knows a cheeky embrace.

The Language of Dust

Dust motes dance like little sprites,
Speaking a language, soft and absurd.
They giggle and twirl in the beams of light,
Whispers of stories without a word.

A broom stands guard, with a knowing gaze,
As it sweeps away secrets long lost.
Caught in the corners, in a lazy daze,
Lies the laughter of dust at no cost.

The windows sigh with tales of the day,
While cobwebs catch jokes we forgot to tell.
In their delicate strands, the laughter will stay,
A faint tickle, like a whimsical spell.

So look to the dust, the jesters so sly,
For they tell of mischief in their soft flight.
Their laughter, a promise, won't say goodbye,
In the language of dust, pure delight.

Threads of Silence

In quiet nooks where shadows loom,
Threads of silence weave a tale.
They tangle and twist, dispelling gloom,
In a blanket that makes the heart exhale.

Each thread a whisper of old deeds done,
Knotted in laughter, stitched with cheer.
Underneath the surface, mischief has spun,
In every corner, a chuckle is near.

A sock hangs lonely, dreaming of pairs,
While the kettle giggles, bubbling with glee.
The pictures on walls share their own stares,
Painting a scene of sweet jubilee.

In this fabric of silence, there's nothing to fear,
Every moment holds a wink and a grin.
So cozy up tight, let the laughter draw near,
As threads of silence gently begin.

Notes of an Echoing Heart

In halls where old echoes play their part,
Every thump beats a funny refrain.
A dog barks back, a rhythmic dart,
Sending giggles through this sweet domain.

The coffee pot hums a jazzy delight,
While chairs chime in with a rattling cheer.
A button rolls, joining the night,
Creating a symphony that we hold dear.

With every creak and sigh of the floor,
Comedic notes rise, echoing wide.
A warm-hearted chuckle is worth so much more,
Than silence playing in hidden pride.

So let the laughter be the song of the space,
Where even the silence adds to the cheer.
In the heart of this home, find your place,
For every echo holds a tale sincere.

Breath of Lingering Twilight

In the corner, a cat wearing a crown,
Loose change dances, it won't settle down.
Lampshades gossip, they lean with delight,
While curtains giggle, in the soft fading light.

A chair keeps its secrets, right by the door,
Of snacks and daydreams, who could ask for more?
Dust bunnies waltz, beneath the old bed,
As mischief whispers, in patterns of red.

The clock throws a party, with hands spinning round,
Tick-tock laughter, that hardly makes a sound.
With socks lost in pairs, and a shoe on a spree,
Each creaky old floorboard knows the history.

An echo of laughter, where memories sway,
In shadows of boredom, we brighten the gray.
With walls painted stories, and dreams in their seams,
Welcome to chaos, where mischief redeems.

Flickers of Forgotten Light

A light bulb flickers, it gives us a show,
It dances and twirls, like it's putting on glow.
The dust in the air does pirouettes too,
While the fridge hums a tune, sounding just like a zoo.

A spider spins webs, catching lost golden dreams,
With whispers of jellybeans and wild, crazy schemes.
The sofa sags low, with a grin on its face,
As the pillows conspire, to throw quite a chase.

The window frames giggle, at neighbors' odd ways,
As the clock's silly tick becomes part of the play.
With each gentle breeze, the curtains start to prance,
While the shadows perform, in a merry old dance.

A laughter erupts from hard-to-reach nooks,
Where stories are hiding, like old dusty books.
In this flickering glow, where the chaos takes flight,
Every moment is silly, in the warm fading light.

Veils of Forgotten Tranquility

In corners, where silence has woven its spell,
The tickle of laughter begins to dispel.
Plants lean in closely, to catch every word,
As the whispering walls giggle, haven't you heard?

A rocking chair sighs, with tales from the past,
While a bird mocks the fridge and its humming so fast.
Shadows twist sideways, in ridiculous ways,
As the dust settles softly, on the end of our days.

The tablecloth flutters, like it's holding a party,
With forks dancing freely, never acting all tardy.
Spilled secrets like confetti, blanket the floor,
As the echoes of chuckles flow right through the door.

Mischief is subtle, in corners and bends,
With stories that twinkle, like mischievous friends.
In veils of reflection, tranquility lies,
Where laughter's the air, and adventure never dies.

Stories that Hang in Stillness

Tales of mischief float, like laundry on lines,
Where socks tell of journeys, and buttons in twines.
A shoe slips on giggles, oh what a delight,
While the brush strokes a portrait of the silliness bright.

In corners of quiet, the cobwebs do spin,
While the old rocking chair plays soft violin.
But oh, what a surprise, when the visitors sneak,
The dust bunnies jump, calling all for a peek.

Whispers of paper, fluttering in dreams,
A paperclip bends, plotting mischievous schemes.
Where the lampstands wink, as shadows align,
And the echo of chuckles becomes simply divine.

Each nook holds a story, where laughter is found,
While the jesting light drapes blankets around.
In stillness, a riddle, where the antics are grand,
And the silence is bursting, as we all take a stand.

Flickering Shadows of Memory

In the corner, dust bunnies dance,
As old ghosts trade their silly glance.
Chairs creak with laughter, wind's gentle sigh,
Whispers tease tales of days gone by.

A cat in the window rolls like a ball,
Chasing the sunbeams that flicker and fall.
Jars on the shelf, filled with dreams of the past,
Giggling secrets, too funny to last.

Memories play in a merry old way,
Wiggling shadows, they come out to play.
Tickling the corners where sunlight can peek,
Making the room feel both funny and bleak.

So cheers to the shadows that flicker and tease,
With every old story, they aim to please.
A tumble of laughter, a flick of the wrist,
In this cozy realm, there's nothing amiss.

Canvas of Quiet Conversations

On the walls, portraits wear silly grins,
As laughter dances where quiet begins.
Trade secrets with echoes at dawn's tender light,
While chairs hold their breath, thrilled by delight.

Painted smiles hide behind timeless frames,
Whispers of nonsense, oh, what are their names?
A canvas alive with the tales that unfold,
In brushstrokes of laughter and giggles untold.

Old clocks chuckle at time with their ticks,
As shadows around them play jumble and mix.
The chatter of silence, it wraps like a shawl,
In this gallery of goofy, we are having a ball!

So gather your thoughts in this intimate space,
Where silly encounters and warmth interlace.
Each glance a chuckle, each sigh a delight,
In this gallery of quiet, everything's bright.

Threads of the Unheard

In the attic, the yarns take flight,
Spinning tales in the fading light.
Whispers of socks hiding under the bed,
Ticklish secrets where no one has tread.

A needle dances, twirls with a grin,
Sewing up laughter where none has been.
Hats that are silly, mittens askew,
Each thread a story, no two are the same hue.

In shadows they weave with a twinkling lark,
Crafting a quilt that ignites a spark.
The fabric of stories, stitched with delight,
Where each little giggle brings warmth to the night.

So let's join the threads, let the mischief begin,
Knit up some joy, let the laughter in.
In the quiet of corners, with joy untold,
Each mischievous stitch a treasure to hold.

A Symphony of Silence

In the hush, a chorus of chuckles arise,
As crickets and candles share sweet lullabies.
The couch lets out giggles with each passing glance,
While curtains do pirouettes, caught in a dance.

A teapot whistles jokes, all brewed with care,
Boiling up laughter that dances in air.
Each room a maestro, conducting with flair,
In the stillness, a ruckus can easily flare.

The whispers of shadows play pranks on the day,
Mimicking sounds in their cheeky ballet.
With each silent note, a punchline unfolds,
Where quiet is funny, and laughter beholds.

So let us embrace this sweet symphony,
Where silence strikes chords of absurdity.
In the playground of quiet, let joy take its place,
With giggles and grins, and the silliest face.

Solitude in the Flickering Light

In a room where whispers play,
Chasing dust while shadows sway,
The cat's on guard, with lazy eyes,
Plotting schemes for midnight pies.

A flickering bulb starts to dance,
It lights the corner, gives a glance,
The chair creaks like an old granddad,
With stories only it has had.

What's that noise? A sock, I swear,
It's crawling off, it's quite a dare!
Against the wall, it makes a break,
To join its friends beneath the flake.

So take a seat, enjoy the play,
Where quiet ghosts come out to sway,
In solitude, the laughter sprouts,
In flickering light, we dance and bounce.

Stories in the Stillness

In corners deep, the stories creep,
A teapot whistles, dreams don't sleep,
The curtains rustle with a grin,
As if they know where jokes begin.

A dust bunny holds a royal court,
With old receipts for their support,
They plan a feast, all crumbs and cheer,
While I just sit and sip my beer.

The clock's hands tick, then play a game,
As time stands still, it feels the same,
A comfy chair gives me a nod,
And whispers tales that seem quite odd.

The stillness hums a tune so light,
While I reflect on laughter bright,
In stories spun from thread and yarn,
The quiet brings a funny charm.

Gentle Shadows of Yesteryear

Gentle shadows stretch and play,
On walls where laughter used to stay,
A picture frame now winks at me,
With smiles from years of jubilee.

Old shoes hang out, don't want to leave,
They dance in place, oh how they weave!
A hat upon the hook nearby,
Catches whispers of the sky.

The passed-down curtains sway in style,
They've seen it all, mile after mile,
With stories tucked in every seam,
They chuckle softly in the dream.

These gentle shadows, they can tease,
With hints of past, they love to please,
In yesteryear's embrace, we find,
A funny tale to share, unwind.

Quiet Cadence of Being

In quiet rooms where echoes dwell,
The laughter rings, oh can't you tell?
The floorboards sing in wooden tune,
As if they know the sun and moon.

With every creak, a joke takes flight,
The fridge hums softly, feels just right,
A sponge, a mop, they spin and sway,
Preparing for a sudsy play.

The shadows flicker, tap their feet,
With every moment, something sweet,
A laugh from here, a chuckle there,
In quiet cadence, joy's laid bare.

So let this space be filled with cheer,
Where simple things can bring us near,
In quiet times, we find the gold,
In funny tales that never get old.

Secrets Beneath Starlit Ceilings

A cat with a hat at the top of the stairs,
Whispers of giggles and old wooden chairs.
The shadows do dance, they hide and they peek,
A tapestry woven of strange tales unique.

Laughter erupts from the creaky floorboards,
As ghosts share their gossip like mischievous lords.
A mouse in a waistcoat is serving up tea,
While socks on the ceiling play tricks, oh so free.

A closet that chuckles, a rug full of grins,
Eerie yet charming, where oddity spins.
Beneath every beam lies a joke in the dark,
Waiting to whisper, to giggle, to spark.

So gather, dear friends, let's embrace all the fun,
In a realm filled with shadows and laughter, we run.
With secrets and stories from corners so bright,
Starlit ceilings will twinkle with joy through the night.

Soft Murmurs of Dusk

Beneath the soft glow of a fading sun,
Rabbits in waistcoats are starting to run.
The dust bunnies giggle as they float in the air,
In whispers of twilight, they spin without care.

Look closely, my friend, at the corner's surprise,
An owl with a monocle, wise and quite sly.
He tells of the days when the tick-tock did race,
Time rolls on laughing, but leaves not a trace.

The shadows tiptoe, with a bounce in their step,
A dance party starts while the old night takes prep.
With moonbeams as partners, they waltz through the gloom,
Soft murmurs of dusk fill the dimly lit room.

So listen, my friend, to the laughter that grows,
As twilight enfolds all our secrets and woes.
From chuckles of dusk to the night's gentle tune,
Embrace all the whimsy beneath the soft moon.

Lullabies of the Unseen

In the corners of rooms where the shadows play low,
Tiny creatures hold concerts that only we know.
Their lullabies echo, a sweet, goofy sound,
As the dust settles softly on all that is found.

The moon grins wide, oh what a sight,
While chairs tell secrets about the last night.
A broom stands guard, with a twitch in its bristle,
Wielding its wisdom like a little old whistle.

As whispers of starlight creep under the door,
A host of delights gently beckons for more.
With tales of the unseen, we gather around,
The laughter of echoes, a joy profound.

So let down your worries, take a moment to see,
In spaces where shadowsw unfold with a glee.
Lullabies ripple through the soft night so bright,
Creating a symphony of whimsy and light.

Shadows in the Attic

In the attic where dust dances, the shadows convene,
With capes made of cobwebs, quite crafty, I mean.
They giggle and plot, planning pranks on the wise,
As shadows of nonsense flit past with a sigh.

An old trunk of treasures, with secrets piled high,
Holds dreams from the past that are cheeky and shy.
The monsters once feared now just want to play,
Chasing dust motes like children, by night and by day.

So hush, little friend, hear the laughter arise,
From corners and rafters, it twinkles and flies.
With shadows as friends, we'll embark on a quest,
To uncover the fun that awaits us, and rest.

For hidden in nooks where the old stories hide,
Are echoes of laughter and joy, side by side.
Shadows in the attic will never grow old,
In their whimsical dance, magic's always retold.

Glistening Dreams of Dust

In corners where the dust bunnies play,
They dance with the light, in a whimsical ray.
Each speck holds a story, a tale to unfold,
Of sock-stealing shadows and treasures of old.

A broom makes a pirate, swashbuckling around,
With feathers for sails, it glides over ground.
Laughter erupts as a cushion clouds land,
In a world where the dust holds a magic so grand.

Piles of forgotten, plush teddy bears snore,
While chairs are the ships that sail out to explore.
Forts made of pillows, with laughter as bait,
In dreams stitched with giggles, we navigate fate.

So raise your glass high, toast the creatures of night,
To dust and its magic, to dreams taking flight.
For each little speck holds a spark of delight,
In this silly abode where our worries take flight.

Nightfall's Gentle Caress

As twilight creeps in with a violet grin,
The moon steals the show, with its mischief akin.
A cat with a top hat begins its grand tour,
While mice on tiny bicycles squeak 'Encore!'

The shadows stretch long, with a tiptoe parade,
Where whispers of giggles in darkness cascade.
Each creak of the floor holds a punchline to share,
As secrets unfold with a flick of the air.

A chair takes a tumble, it's unsure if to stay,
As slippers conspire to lead it astray.
In the blanket fort castle, one queen makes a vow,
With a corny old joke, who will giggle now?

So revel in chaos, in mischief's embrace,
Where shadows and giggles find their own place.
For nightfall is laughter, a whimsical guise,
In the dance of the dreamers, where silliness lies.

Cracks Of Light and Dusty Air

Through cracks in the wall, sunlight beams bold,
A disco of dust motes, a sight to behold.
They twirl and they spin in an eerie ballet.
While shadows anxiously plot their new play.

The old chair croaks loud, a grand joke to tell,
It squeaks of old tales and adages swell.
The floorboards groan softly, with secrets they share,
As the tired, dusty curtains cool down in the air.

Lampshades peek down with a knowing old smile,
As the cat makes a leap, "Oh, it's been a while!"
In each little corner, where giggles expand,
Lives a world made of laughter, just waiting, unplanned.

So breathe in the charm of this place filled with cheer,
The dusty old treasures, they're always so near.
For in every warm glow, where memories float,
There's humor tangled up in a forgotten coat.

Whispers of the Forgotten Garden

In the garden of whispers, where mischief has sprouted,
The squirrels share secrets, all nicely routed.
A gnome with a smirk offers wisdom like wine,
While flowers exchange puns in the bright sunshine.

A bird with a bowtie sings tunes of delight,
While mushrooms hold parties that last through the night.
The hedges conspire, they're quite full of schemes,
In the realm of the garden, where laughter it gleams.

The trees tell tall tales, their branches a stage,
While crickets provide rhythms to turn every page.
Sunflowers nod knowingly, bows on their heads,
As laughter erupts in this land of sweet threads.

So come join the jesters, and twirl in the breeze,
Where the echoes of chuckles float softly with ease.
In this haven of giggles, the heart beats with glee,
As whispers of joy fill the air, wild and free.

Echoes of a Whispered Age

In a nook where dust does play,
A ghostly cat will sway.
With every creak and moan,
It steals my favorite throne.

A portrait smiles with cheeky glee,
Winks at me, oh what a spree!
The chandeliers begin to dance,
In this odd, enchanting trance.

An old clock strikes, but who can tell?
Time seems caught inside a spell.
I chuckle at this merry plight,
When shadows join the silly fight.

The echoes laugh without a care,
As dust bunnies float in midair.
I raise my teacup to the crew,
In this jaunt, it's all so true!

Ethereal Embrace of Abandon

In corners where the whispers dwell,
Cobwebs weave a secret spell.
The chairs gossip, old and wise,
While sunlight dances, oh how it flies!

Forgotten toys with tales to share,
Beneath the stairs, they linger there.
With tattered hats and mismatched socks,
They plot their games and silly mocks.

A breeze swirls in with such delight,
Tickling curtains, oh what a sight!
Each rustle seems to laugh and play,
In this place where shadows sway.

The echoes giggle through the halls,
As laughter bounces off the walls.
In carefree jest, they all unite,
In this age of whimsical light.

Quiet Reveries Beneath the Eaves

Up in the loft, a sneaky breeze,
Catches my thoughts, like honeyed bees.
A chair with a squeak plays the fool,
As I settle in, all nice and cool.

Worn-out shoes with stories old,
Whisper secrets, brave and bold.
With every shuffle, every trudge,
They seem to say, "Don't hold a grudge!"

An old gramophone starts to croon,
Tunes from a long-forgotten June.
Laughter echoes, light as air,
In this reverie, I freely dare.

With shadows peeking, sly and bright,
I chuckle softly, what a sight!
In this realm of dreams and mirth,
I find the magic of rebirth.

Traces of a Gentle Presence

In the attic, dust settles down,
On boots that once roamed this town.
With every step, they whisper clear,
Of days gone by, oh how they cheer!

A lamp shakes off its dreary gloom,
Flickers alive in this cozy room.
As shadows dance along the wall,
I've got to grin; I'll heed their call.

Unseen guests invite a laugh,
In this cozy aftermath.
With ghostly giggles in the air,
They tumble forth, without a care.

A puzzle waits, pieces misplaced,
Yet joy abounds with all the haste.
These traces twirl in joyful glee,
Their laughter echoes, wild and free!

Murmurs of a Wandering Mind

In a dusty nook, a sock does hide,
Under the bed, where memories bide.
A chair squeaks tales of old wooden glee,
And whispers of ghosts that laugh with the bee.

Curtains dance as the wind straightens hair.
An old cat plops down, she doesn't care.
With strange little pauses for dust motes to play,
Each hour a giggle, oh what a day!

The clock strikes twelve, it's a bit of a joke,
For time is a riddle, a soft, merry poke.
A potato chip dreams of being a fry,
In this comical realm, time just won't fly.

So laugh with the shadows, they beckon us here,
With tales of a chair that once held a seer.
The mind wanders freely, with no need for maps,
In a world that spins round with giggles and laughs.

Tides of Lingering Light

Light tiptoes in, as day starts to yawn,
The fridge hums a tune, it's got magic drawn.
Lamps flicker playfully, casting their glow,
While old photos chuckle, like they're in the know.

A teapot whistles with stories untold,
Of adventures with muffins, both brave and bold.
The couch cushions giggle, they're snug and tight,
As if they are whispers of a sweet pastry fight.

The shadows commence their goofy parade,
Dancing on walls, in spontaneous charade.
A spoon winks softly, invites laughter nearby,
While candles engage in their waxy sigh.

The antics abound, and we can't help but cheer,
For life in this space is delightfully sheer.
Like tides of a humor that carries us high,
We float on the chuckles that twinkle the sky.

The Soft Embrace of Twilight

Twilight arrives with a playful grin,
The sky dons its purple, let the fun begin!
Fireflies gather, like stars come to play,
While crickets perform in a band of cabaret.

A cat on a fence gives a dubious stare,
While shadows cavort with a dance full of flair.
The evening sighs soft as it tucks the sun,
In a blanket of giggles, the day's almost done.

Trees whisper secrets, their leaves shimmy down,
As if making jokes, without any frown.
Lamps flicker on one by one, sheer delight,
Painting the world in soft hues of night.

So, laugh with the dusk, let your worries go,
In this gentle twilight, let the joy overflow.
For every soft shadow has a jest up its sleeve,
Just waiting for viewers who're ready to believe.

Paths of Unfollowed Journeys

In corners untraveled, mischief will sprout,
With socks entwined, that's what it's about.
Frog hats and capes made of fluff and of thread,
Strut down hallways where soft echoes tread.

A wobbly table may tell you a tale,
Of crumbs from a party where guests turned pale.
Each step is a riddle, in sneakers or crocs,
And laughter is mirrored on old wooden clocks.

The fridge opens wide for the snack-hungry souls,
Where pickles and chocolate form comical roles.
Jars of strange veggies giggle, take flight,
Inviting all wanderers to taste their delight.

Through paths untraveled, with humor as guide,
We dance with the shadows that giggle and glide.
For every misstep is just a new game,
In this land of the jolly, we're never the same.

Reflections in Dusty Mirrors

In corners hide the sneaky dust,
Where socks and shoes blend, you can trust.
The mirror winks, a sly old friend,
Whispers secrets that never end.

A cat's tail sways with regal grace,
While chairs conspire to take their place.
The clock laughs loud, it's out of tune,
Time confesses to a cartoon moon.

The shadows play hide and seek,
Mischief laughs, but never speaks.
Old photos grin and roll their eyes,
As they plot new, silly goodbyes.

The laughter echoes, soft and bright,
In every nook, a cheeky sight.
The whispers float on velvet air,
Shake off the dust, if you dare!

Lullabies of an Empty Room

The bed creaks low, a husky tune,
As pillows chat with the absent moon.
Curtains twirl in gentle glee,
Tickling whispers of ghosts that be.

A forgotten toy begins to hum,
As shadows dance and softly come.
Chairs lean back, become a throne,
While the fridge chuckles, all alone.

Dust bunnies gather, form a band,
They tap their feet, take a stand.
Posters giggle, colors bright,
As the stars peek in, just for spite.

In this stillness, laughter blooms,
From hidden places, into rooms.
A symphony of ghosts may sing,
As sleepy corners find their spring.

The Unseen Footsteps of Time

Footsteps whisper on the floor,
As socks escape from every drawer.
The hallway giggles, creaks with pride,
While clocks do tango, time's not wide.

Walls bear witness, tales unfold,
Of sock puppets and jokes retold.
A ghostly hiccup fills the air,
Shake up the dust, eliminate despair!

The shadows leap like playful sprites,
Tickling walls in moonlit nights.
A purple chair, a playful jest,
Bears secrets deep, now put to rest.

Each photo smiles, a silly pose,
In memories, the laughter grows.
Time tiptoes lightly, so sublime,
As echoes dance, defying rhyme.

Ghosts of Laughter Long Past

In corners, giggles softly cling,
As echoes of the past take wing.
The old piano plays a tune,
While dust collects like a greedy spoon.

Whirligigs spin in a playful race,
While memories twirl around the space.
A rocking chair sings a lullaby,
To all who listen, with a sigh.

Old shoes gossip, worn and wise,
Whispering tales of great surprise.
A storyteller in every creak,
Speaks of laughter, old but sleek.

These walls hold jokes and playful pranks,
Laughter shared among the ranks.
In shadows bright, a past alive,
Where ghosts of joy do laugh and thrive.

Hushed Footsteps on Lonesome Floors

In the hallway, a creak and a squeak,
A ghost in slippers, so soft, so meek.
It tiptoes around, a mischievous sprite,
Playing hide and seek with the moonlight.

Dust bunnies giggle in corners unseen,
While shadows dance, oh what a scene!
The echo of laughter, a giggle, a sigh,
As the cat observes with one lazy eye.

A phantom's haunting, but what's the rush?
He just wants to join in on the hush.
With every step, a sneeze might erupt,
From a hidden nook where a spirit is cupped.

Whispers and chuckles fill empty rooms,
Where the air is thick like sweet perfume.
A tapestry woven with tales so quaint,
In this abode where the quiet can't wait.

Veil of Faded Memories

In dusty corners, jokes are stored tight,
Where laughter loves to escape from the night.
A picture hangs askew on the wall,
Poking fun at the way it took a fall.

Old sock puppets plot by the light,
Reminiscing of parties that lasted all night.
With stories shared, they wiggle and twist,
Each memory a giggle, too good to resist.

Cobwebs cling like secrets they know,
Of days filled with play, and the times they let go.
The ghosts pull a prank just for fun,
Leaving shadows of joy when the day is done.

So, raise a glass to the past we adore,
With whispers that linger forevermore.
The veil may be faded, but laughter's still bright,
In the realm of sweet memories that dance in the night.

Secrets Between the Walls

Cracks in the plaster tell stories unseen,
Of mischief and mayhem that once filled the scene.
A squirrel once scolded a spider for fun,
While whispers of chaos from old jokes would run.

Behind painted panels, where secrets reside,
A riddle or two, let the fun coincide.
The mice have a clubhouse, complete with a sign,
That claims "No humans allowed, we're just fine!"

Tick-tock goes the clock, a comedic chime,
As ghouls with bad puns take their turn in prime.
They chuckle and snicker at midnight's delight,
Creating a cacophony to frighten the night.

So listen close, to the whispers and sighs,
For laughter is hiding where silence complies.
Between the walls where the shadows might melt,
Lies a treasure of joy that always is felt.

Traces of a Timeless Evening

The moon peeks in with a grin, what a sight,
As shadows play tag in the soft silver light.
A chair creaks softly, a sneeze from the muse,
As memories shuffle, each one with its ruse.

Old records spin with a pop and a crack,
While echoes of laughter bring spirits back.
Each note a reminder of joy from the past,
With dancing footsteps that seem to outlast.

Time travelers peek through the open door,
Whispering tales that beg to explore.
With a wink and a nod, they share jokes anew,
In the twilight's embrace, where the night turns blue.

So let the evening boast its playful disguise,
As old memories sparkle like stars in the skies.
In this timeless retreat, where spirits may roam,
The laughter of shadows returns, always home.

Candles Flickering in the Twilight

Candles dance and flicker bright,
Casting shadows in the night.
A cat trips over an unseen shoe,
While mice snicker at the view.

Wobbly chairs begin to creak,
As ghosts gather for a sneak peek.
They whisper jokes, so silly, so light,
While laughter echoes, oh what a sight!

A chandelier laden with cobwebs sways,
Mocking the dust bunnies' ballet.
It's a party in this dim-lit dream,
Where nothing is ever what it seems.

So grab a seat, pull up a drink,
Join the fun, take a moment to think.
In this quirky realm of shadows' play,
We laugh at mishaps, come what may!

Tread Softly in This Silence

Tiptoe through this quiet space,
Where time dances with a goofy grace.
A mouse in boots struts with flair,
Leaving tiny prints everywhere.

The clock ticks loudly, what a jest!
It tells the world to take a rest.
But here, a sock puppet steals the show,
As the silence takes on a playful glow.

Whispers to walls that can't respond,
Creating laughter that free bounds.
We tell our secrets to the night,
With giggles bouncing left and right.

In the stillness, chaos creeps,
The floorboards groan and laugh as they sleep.
So tread softly, share a grin,
For in this place, the fun begins!

Whispers in the Dust

In corners deep, the dust lays thick,
Holding secrets, like a magic trick.
A spider wearing a tiny hat,
Throws a party for this old pet cat.

The brooms stand by, looking awfully neat,
Avoiding the dust, they'd rather not meet
But they join in, shuffling about,
As dust motes twirl and dance throughout.

A story emerges from an old shoe,
Say the whispers, 'It's quite overdue!'
For the socks discuss their sock-less plight,
As they reminisce on their laundry knight.

So listen close, to the murmured joke,
Of dust's great wisdom, softly bespoke.
In this light-hearted gathering, so antique,
Laughter breathes where silence seems bleak.

Echoes of Forgotten Corners

In forgotten corners, echoes play,
Of laughter from a time of sway.
Where once stood chairs for dances grand,
Now hover shadows, hand in hand.

A broom leans close, it knows the score,
Of dust bunnies plotting what's in store.
They giggle softly, 'Let's make a mess!'
As they plan their next dust-distress.

Footsteps shuffle, the echoes blend,
With whispers of secrets that never end.
A doorknob chuckles, 'I've been unlocked!'
While the moon beams down, a sneak attack.

So tip back on your creaky chair,
And let the echoes drift through the air.
For in these corners, the laughter's loud,
In a home where shadows form a crowd.

Solace of Silent Hallways

In hallways where whispers play,
Cats chase ghosts in a lazy sway.
Walls are painted with laughter's glow,
While creaky floors have stories to show.

Light flickers like a silly dance,
Chasing shadows, they take a chance.
A vase with a grin, always askew,
Dances with dust, it's quite the view.

In corners, odd socks start to feud,
Debating which one's more subdued.
Old chairs chuckle under the strain,
As unseen guests play a lighthearted game.

So join the jests in this quirky place,
Where time is a jest, and smiles embrace.
Flip a coin for laughter or glee,
In this plush realm of oddity.

Dreams in Dusty Nooks

In dusty nooks where dreams take flight,
A rubber chicken entertains at night.
Pillows giggle with every squeeze,
As memories flutter like autumn leaves.

Jars of jellybeans hold court with glee,
While mismatched socks throw a jubilee.
Whispers of popcorn pop with delight,
Encouraging the critters to sing all night.

Cobwebs weave a tale of cheer,
Where shadows waltz and tickle your ear.
A clock ticks in a playful rhyme,
Counting laughs instead of time.

So peer into the corners so grand,
Where silly secrets take a stand.
In the quietest places, joy persists,
As autumn leaves dance in whimsical mist.

Murmurs of the Midnight Wind

The midnight wind hums a tune,
Tickling branches, a playful swoon.
It swirls around with a cheeky grin,
Enticing owls to join in the din.

Crickets chirp jokes in starlit cheer,
While fireflies twinkle, lending an ear.
The moon cracks a joke, it lights up the scene,
As if to say life's sweet and green.

Branches clap hands in the cool of the night,
While shadows recite in ghosts of delight.
The air's filled with giggles and lighthearted play,
As the wind whisks our cares far away.

So listen closely to the whispers around,
For laughter in silence is truly profound.
Let the night carry you on laughter's wings,
For joy in the shadows is what midnight brings.

Reflections in the Gloom

In the gloom where reflections lie,
A lumpy sofa sighs with a try.
Mirrors wear hats, quite askew,
Crafting companions all painted blue.

Candles chuckle, flickering bright,
While shadows skedaddle, delighting in fright.
The rug huffs a tune underfoot,
With a tickle attack, it giggles and puts.

Old portraits wink with mischief and charm,
A dog in a bowtie, ready to disarm.
The clock on the wall keeps a comical beat,
Marking the moments with little retreat.

So stroll through the gloom, where oddities gleam,
In this playful maze, find a new dream.
For laughter's the light that brightens the night,
In reflections of humor, everything's bright.

www.ingramcontent.com/pod-product-compliance
Lightning Source LLC
Chambersburg PA
CBHW060134230426
43661CB00003B/413